95 Bodybuilder Meal and Shake Recipes to Improve Muscle Growth

Less Work and Faster Results

By

Joseph Correa

Certified Sports Nutritionist

COPYRIGHT

© 2016 Finibi Inc

All rights reserved

Reproduction or translation of any part of this work beyond that permitted by section 107 or 108 of the 1976 United States Copyright Act without the permission of the copyright owner is unlawful.

This publication is designed to provide accurate and authoritative information in regard to the subject matter covered. It is sold with the understanding that neither the author nor the publisher is engaged in rendering medical advice. If medical advice or assistance is needed, consult with a doctor. This book is considered a guide and should not be used in any way detrimental to your health. Consult with a physician before starting this nutritional plan to make sure it's right for you.

ACKNOWLEDGEMENTS

The realization and success of this book could not have been possible without my family.

95 Bodybuilder Meal and Shake Recipes to Improve Muscle Growth

Less Work and Faster Results

By

Joseph Correa

Certified Sports Nutritionist

CONTENTS

Copyright

Acknowledgements

About The Author

Introduction

Bodybuilder Meal and Shake Calendar

Bodybuilder Meal Recipes

Bodybuilder Shake Recipes

Other Great Titles by This Author

ABOUT THE AUTHOR

As a certified sports nutritionist and professional athlete, I firmly believe that proper nutrition will help you reach your goals faster and effectively. My knowledge and experience has helped me live healthier throughout the years and which I have shared with family and friends. The more you know about eating and drinking healthier, the sooner you will want to change your life and eating habits.

Being successful in controlling your weight is important as it will improve all aspects of your life.

Nutrition is a key part in the process of getting in better shape and that's what this book is all about.

INTRODUCTION

95 Bodybuilder Meal and Shake Recipes to Improve Muscle Growth will help you increase the amount of protein you consume per day to help increase muscle mass. The meal and shake recipes, along with the calendar, will help you increase muscle mass in an accelerated and organized manner so that you can schedule what you eat and when.

Being too busy to eat right can sometimes become a problem and that's why this book will save you time and help nourish your body to achieve the goals you want. Make sure you know what you're eating by preparing it yourself or having someone prepare it for you.

This book will help you to:

-Gain muscle mass fast.

-Have more energy during training.

-Naturally accelerate Your Metabolism to build more muscle.

-Improve your digestive system.

Joseph Correa is a certified sports nutritionist and a professional athlete.

Bodybuilder Meal and Shake

Calendar

Week 1

Day 1:

Early Riser Breakfast

Snack: Blueberry Yogurt

Tuna Burger and Salad

Snack: Cherry Tomatoes with Cottage Cheese

Mexican Style Protein Bowl

Day 2:

Blueberry Lemon Pancakes

Snack: Avocado on Toast

Spicy Beefsteak Kebabs

Snack: Apple and Peanut Butter

Mediterranean Fish

Day 3:

Power Bowl

Snack: Yogurt with Tropical Fruit

Stuffed Chicken Breast with Brown Rice

Snack: Bell Pepper with Cottage Cheese

Vegan Friendly Dinner

Day 4:

Almond Milk Smoothie

Snack: Cup of Popcorn

Pancetta-wrapped Pollock with Potatoes

Snack: Yogurt with Dried Goji Berries

Garlicky Hummus

Day 5

Greek Yogurt with Flaxseeds and Apple

Snack: Rice Cake with Peanut Butter

Baked Salmon with Grilled Asparagus

Snack: Celery Sticks with Goat Cheese and Green Olives

Chicken with Avocado Salad

Day 6:

Breakfast 'Pizza'

Snack: Greek Yogurt with Strawberries

Chicken Caesar Wraps

Snack: Roasted Chickpeas

Hot Cod

Day 7:

Bell Pepper Rings with 'Frit Grits'

Snack: Nut Mix

Beef and Broccoli Noodles

Snack: Ham and Celery Sticks

Arugula Chicken Salad

Week 2

Day 1:

Whey Protein Muffins

Snack: Avocado on Toast

Shrimp and Zucchini Linguine Pasta Salad

Snack: Apple and Peanut Butter

Tofu Burger

Day 2:

Mexican Mocha Breakfast

Snack: Yogurt with Dried Goji Berries

Trout with Potato Salad

Snack: Cup of Popcorn

Chicken with Pineapple and Bell Peppers

Day 3:

Smoked Salmon and Avocado with Toast

Snack: Cherry Tomatoes with Cottage Cheese

Spiced Chicken

Snack: Blueberry Yogurt

Grilled Mushroom and Zucchini Burger

Day 4:

Fruit and Peanut Butter Smoothie

Snack: Roasted Chickpeas

Mexican Bean Chili

Snack: Greek Yogurt with Strawberries

Sweet and Sour Chicken

Day 5:

Protein-packed Scramble

Snack: Bell pepper with Cottage Cheese

Turkey Meatloaf with Whole Wheat Couscous

Snack: Yogurt with Tropical Fruit

Dijon Mustard Halibut

Day 6:

Pumpkin Pie Protein Pancakes

Snack: Ham and Celery Sticks

Mediterranean Rice

Snack: Nut Mix

Tuna Melt

Day 7:

Tuna Stuffed Bell Peppers

Snack: Celery Sticks with Goat Cheese and Green Olives

Beef Meatball Pasta with Spinach

Snack: Rice Cake with Peanut Butter

Sushi Bowl

Week 3

Day 1:

High-protein Oatmeal

Snack: Cup of Popcorn

Stuffed Eggs with Pita Bread

Snack: Apple and Peanut Butter

Tray Bake Chicken

Day 2:

Early Riser Breakfast

Snack: Avocado on Toast

Beef and Broccoli Noodles

Snack: Yogurt with Dried Goji Berries

Garlicky Hummus

Day 3:

Power Bow

Snack: Greek Yogurt with Strawberries

Chicken Caesar Wraps

Snack: Cherry Tomatoes with Goat Cheese

Mediterranean Fish

Day 4:

Blueberry Lemon Pancakes

Snack: Roasted Chickpeas

Baked Salmon with Grilled Asparagus

Snack: Blueberry Yogurt

Arugula Chicken Salad

Day 5:

Greek Yogurt with Flaxseeds and Apple

Snack: Ham and Celery Sticks

Tuna Burger and Salad

Snack: Yogurt with Tropical Fruit

Chicken with Avocado Salad

Day 6:

Bell Pepper Rings with 'Frit Grits'

Snack: Bell Peppers with Cottage Cheese

Stuffed Chicken Breast with Brown Rice

Snack: Nut Mix

Hot Cod

Day 7:

Almond Milk Smoothie

Snack: Rice Cake with Peanut Butter

Spicy Beefsteak Kebabs

Snack: Celery Sticks with Goat Cheese and Green Olives

Mexican Style Protein Bowl

Week 4

Day 1:

Breakfast 'Pizza'

Snack: Greek Yogurt with Strawberries

Pancetta-wrapped Pollock with Potatoes

Snack: Cup of Popcorn

Vegan Friendly Dinner

Day 2:

Mexican Mocha Breakfast

Snack: Cherry Tomatoes with Cottage Cheese

Mediterranean Rice

Snack: Apple and Peanut Butter

Grilled Mushroom and Zucchini Burger

Day 3:

Fruit and Peanut Butter Smoothie

Snack: Avocado on Toast

Shrimp and Zucchini Linguine Pasta Salad

Snack: Blueberry Yogurt

Sweet and Sour Chicken

Day 4:

Pumpkin Pie Protein Pancakes

Snack: Yogurt with Dried Goji Berries

Spiced Chicken

Snack: Roasted Chickpeas

Dijon Mustard Halibut

Day 5:

Smoked Salmon and Avocado with Toast

Snack: Ham and Celery Sticks

Beef Meatball Pasta with Spinach

Snack: Nut Mix

Tofu Burger

Day 6:

High-protein Oatmeal

Snack: Bell Peppers with Cottage Cheese

Mexican Bean Chili

Snack: Yogurt with Tropical Fruit

Sushi Bowl

Day 7:

Protein-packed Scramble

Snack: Rice Cake with Peanut Butter

Trout with Potato Salad

Snack: Greek Yogurt with Strawberries

Tray Bake Chicken

2 extra days for a full month:

Day 1:

Whey Protein Muffins

Snack: Celery Sticks with Goat Cheese and Green Olives

Turkey Meatloaf with Whole Wheat Couscous

Snack: Apple and Peanut Butter

Tuna Melt

Day 2:

Tuna Stuffed Bell Peppers

Snack: Blueberry Yogurt

Stuffed Eggs with Pita Bread

Snack: Nut Mix

Chicken with Pineapple and Bell Peppers

BODYBUILDER MEAL RECIPES

BREAKFAST

1. Early Riser Breakfast

Snap your body out of a catabolic state and into a muscle-building one with this high-protein, high-carb oven-cooked breakfast. The grapefruit and asparagus make sure you get more than half a day's worth of vitamin C.

Ingredients (1serving):

6 egg whites

½ cup cooked quinoa and brown rice mix

3 asparagus spears, sliced

½ pink grapefruit

1 small red bell pepper, sliced

1 scoop flavorless whey protein powder

1 clove garlic, crushed

olive oil spray

pepper, salt

Prep time: 10 min

Cooking time: 15-20 min

Preparation:

Heat the oven to 200C fan/ gas 6. Lightly spray a cast iron skillet with olive oil.

In a medium bowl, whisk the egg whites with a pinch of salt and pepper until frothy.

Add the cooked brown rice and quinoa to the skillet; pour in the egg whites then the asparagus pieces and the bell pepper slices.

Bake in the oven for 15-20 min or until the eggs are cooked.

Nutritional value per serving: 407kcal, 52g protein, 40g carbs (5g fiber, 8g sugar), 2g fat, 15% calcium, 12% iron, 19% magnesium, 26% vitamin A, 63% vitamin C, 48% vitamin K, 12% vitamin B1, 69% vitamin B2, 26% vitamin B9.

2. Power Bowl

A breakfast with an appropriate name, the power bowl combines high in protein egg whites with energy fueling oatmeal. The walnuts add healthy fats and the honey tops everything with a bit of sweetness.

Ingredients (1 serving):

6 egg whites

½ cup instant oatmeal, cooked

1/8 cup walnuts

¼ cup berries

1 teaspoon raw honey

Cinnamon

Prep time: 10 min

Cooking time: 5 min

Preparation:

Whisk the egg whites until frothy then cook them in a skillet on low heat.

Combine the oatmeal and the egg whites in a bowl; add the cinnamon and raw honey and mix.

Top with berries, banana and walnuts.

Nutritional value per serving: 344kcal, 30g protein, 33g carbs (3g fiber, 23g sugar), 11g fat (2 saturated), 10% iron, 15% magnesium, 10% vitamin B1, 11% vitamin B2, 15% vitamin B5.

3. Tuna Stuffed Bell Peppers

This is a quick and nutritious recipe that provides a massive amount of B12. High in protein, tuna is an excellent breakfast option for muscle building and if you want to add some carbs to your meal, a piece of whole wheat toast is a great choice.

Ingredients (2 servings):

2 cans of tuna in water (185g), half drained

3 hard-boiled eggs

1 spring onion, finely chopped

5 small pickles, diced

salt, pepper

4 bell peppers, halved, with the seeds cleaned

Prep time: 5 min

Cooking time: 10 min

Preparation:

Combine the tuna, eggs, spring onion, pickles and seasoning in a food processor and mix until smooth.

Fill the halves of the bell peppers with the composition and serve.

Nutritional value per serving: 480kcal, 46g protein, 16g fat (4g saturated), 8g carbs (2g fiber, 4g sugar), 28%

magnesium, 94% vitamin A, 400% vitamin C, 12% vitamin E, 67% vitamin K, 18% vitamin B1, 32% vitamin B2, 90% vitamin B3, 20% vitamin B5, 56% vitamin B6, 18% vitamin B9, 284% vitamin B12.

4. Greek Yogurt with Flaxseeds and Apple

Branch out from the traditional egg white muscle-building breakfast and try some high-protein Greek Yogurt flavored with apple. Use whole flaxseeds to maximize your fiber intake and keep them in water overnight to get them soft and easily digestible.

Ingredients (1 serving):

1 cup Greek yogurt

1 apple, thinly sliced

2 tablespoons flaxseeds

¼ teaspoon cinnamon

1 teaspoon Stevia

A sprinkle of salt

Prep time: 5 min

Cooking time: 45 min

Preparation:

Preheat the oven to 190C fan/ gas 5. Place the apple slices in a non-stick pan, sprinkle them with cinnamon, Stevia and a dash of salt, cover them and bake for 45 min/ until tender. Remove them from the oven and allow them to cool for 30 min.

Place the Greek yogurt in a bowl then top with apples and flaxseeds and serve.

Nutritional value per serving: 422kcal, 22g protein, 39g carbs (7g fiber, 22 g sugar), 21g fat (8 g saturated), 14% calcium, 22% magnesium, 14% vitamin C, 24% vitamin B1, 13% vitamin B12.

5. Bell Pepper Rings with 'Fit Grits'

A tasty and special looking meal, the bell pepper rings with 'Fit Grits' fuel your muscles and give you enough energy to power through your day. Full of color and nutrients, this breakfast is high in vitamin B1.

Ingredients (1 serving):

6 egg whites

2 eggs

¼ cup brown rice farina

1 cup raw spinach

½ green bell pepper

1 cup of cherry tomatoes

olive oil spray

salt, pepper

Prep time: 10 min

Cooking time: 15 min

Preparation:

Whisk the egg whites with a pinch of salt and pepper until frothy. Heat some oil in a non-stick frying pan and cook the egg whites and farina. Add the spinach, mix together and cook until the spinach has wilted.

Lightly spray a skillet with olive oil and set on medium heat. Cut the bell peppers horizontally to create 2 rings, place them in the skillet and crack the eggs inside the bell peppers. Let them cook until the eggs turn white.

Place the egg-farina mixture and cooked pepper rings on a plate and serve with cherry tomatoes.

Nutritional value per serving : 495kcal, 45g protein, 45g carbs (3g fiber, 7g sugar), 11g fat (3g saturated), 9% calcium, 14% iron, 20% magnesium, 35% vitamin A, 32% vitamin C, 91% vitamin B2, 22% vitamin B5, 12% vitamin B6, 15% vitamin B12.

6. Almond Milk Smoothie

10 minutes is all you need to fix this high in vitamin D and B1 almond milk smoothie. You can fix a big batch and keep it in the freezer making this smoothie a perfect option for a quick breakfast to go.

Ingredients (2 serving):

1 cup almond milk

1 cup frozen mixed berries

1 cup spinach

1 scoop banana flavored protein powder

1 tablespoon chia seeds

Prep time: 10 min

No cooking

Preparation:

Mix all the ingredients in a blender until smooth, pour into 2 glasses and serve.

Nutritional value per serving: 295kcal, 26g protein, 32g carbs (4g fiber, 13g sugar), 9g fat, 40% calcium, 20% iron, 12% magnesium, 50% vitamin A, 40% vitamin C, 25% vitamin D, 57% vitamin E, 213% vitamin B1, 18% vitamin B9.

7. Pumpkin Pie Protein Pancakes

Forget about flour and try oat pancakes with a delicious addition of fresh pumpkin. Topple some calorie-free syrup and enjoy a high-protein breakfast that tastes as good as a cheat meal.

Ingredients (1 serving):

1/3 cup old-fashioned oats

¼ cup pumpkin

½ cup egg whites

1 scoop cinnamon protein powder

½ teaspoon cinnamon

olive oil spray

Prep time: 5 min

Cooking time: 5 min

Preparation:

Mix all the ingredients together in a bowl. Spray a medium-sized skillet with olive oil then place on medium heat.

Pour in the batter, and once you see tiny bubbles appear on the top of the pancake, flip. When each side is golden, remove the pancake and serve.

Nutritional value per serving: 335kcal, 39g protein, 37g carbs (6g fiber, 1 g sugar), 6g fat, 14% calcium, 15% iron, 26% magnesium, 60% vitamin A, 26% vitamin B1, 37% vitamin B2, 10% vitamin B5, 31% vitamin B6.

8. High-protein Oatmeal

Lasso in a hearty helping of carbs that will keep you satiated for hours, while the protein powder and almonds will deliver a protein-packed start to your day. If you prefer you oatmeal with a fruity taste, use banana flavored protein powder.

Ingredients (1 serving):

2 packets of instant oatmeal (28g packet)

¼ cup ground almonds

1 scoop of vanilla flavored whey protein powder

1 tablespoon cinnamon

Prep time: 5 min

Cooking time: 5 min

Preparation:

Pour the instant oatmeal into a bowl, mix with the protein powder and cinnamon. Add hot water and mix. Top with crushed almonds and serve.

Nutritional value per serving: 436kcal, 33g protein, 45g carbs (10g fiber, 4g sugar), 15g fat (1g saturated), 17% calcium, 19% iron, 37% magnesium, 44% vitamin E, 21% vitamin B1, 21% vitamin B2.

9. Protein-packed Scramble

Feed your muscles and push through an intense workout with this 51g protein meal. These scrambled egg whites with vegetables and turkey sausage have the added value of being packed with carbs and overall high amounts of vitamins.

Ingredients (1 serving):

8 egg whites

2 link turkey sausages, chopped

1 large onion, diced

1 cup red bell peppers, diced

2 tomatoes, diced

2 cups raw spinach, chopped

1 teaspoon olive oil

salt and pepper

Prep time: 10 min

Cooking time: 10-15 min

Preparation:

Whisk the egg whites with a pinch of salt and pepper until frothy, then set aside.

Heat the oil in a large non-stick pan, drizzle the onions and peppers and sauté until they are tender. Season with salt and pepper. Add the turkey sausage and cook until it is golden brown then lower the heat and add the egg whites and scramble.

When the eggs are almost done, add the tomato and spinach, cook for 2 min and serve.

Nutritional value per serving: 475kcal, 51g protein, 37g carbs (10g fiber, 18g sugar), 10g fat (2g saturated), 14% calcium, 23% iron, 37% magnesium, 255% vitamin A, 516% vitamin C, 25% vitamin E, 397% vitamin K, 22% vitamin B1, 112% vitamin B2, 29% vitamin B3, 19% vitamin B5, 51% vitamin B6, 65% vitamin B9.

10. Fruit and Peanut Butter Smoothie

What better way to get your day's worth of calcium than with this strawberry flavored smoothie? High in minerals, vitamins, protein and energy fueling carbs, this smoothie is a perfect way to kick-start your day.

Ingredients (1 serving):

15 medium-sized strawberries

1 1/3 tablespoons peanut butter

85g tofu

½ cup fat free yogurt

¾ cup skim milk

1 scoop protein powder

8 ice cubes

Prep time: 5min

No cooking

Preparation:

Pour the milk into the blender then the yogurt and the rest of the ingredients. Blend until mixture is completely blended and frothy. Pour into a glass and serve.

Nutritional value per serving: 472kcal, 45g protein, 40g carbs (6g fiber, 31g sugar), 13g fat (4g saturated), 110% calcium, 35% iron, 27% magnesium, 30% vitamin A, 190% vitamin C, 11% vitamin E, 13% vitamin B1, 24% vitamin B2, 10% vitamin B5, 18% vitamin B6, 17% vitamin B9, 12% vitamin B12.

11. Whey Protein Muffins

With a healthy dose of oats and a serving of chocolate whey protein powder, these muffins are a great breakfast alternative to regular oats. Paired with a glass of milk, this meal makes sure that you get a good amount of calcium and vitamin D to go with the nice protein and carbs serving.

Ingredients (4 muffins-2 servings):

1 cup rolled oats

1 large whole egg

5 large egg whites

½ scoop chocolate whey protein powder

olive oil spray

2 cups of low fat milk, to serve

Prep time: 2 min

Cooking time: 15 min

Preparation:

Preheat the oven to 190C fan/ gas 5.

Blend all the ingredients together for 30s. Spray the muffin tin with olive oil then batter up into four muffins. Place in the oven for 15 min.

Remove from the oven, let them cool and serve with the glass of milk.

Nutritional value per serving (includes milk): 330kcal, 28g protein, 37g carbs (9g fiber, 13g sugar), 6g fat (5g saturated), 37% calcium, 22% iron, 19% magnesium, 12% vitamin A, 34% vitamin D, 44% vitamin B1, 66% vitamin B2, 25% vitamin B5, 11% vitamin B6, 24% vitamin B12.

12. Smoked Salmon and Avocado with Toast

Are you in for a tough workout and low on time? It only takes 5 min to piece together this savory breakfast. Both the salmon and avocado are high in healthy acids and this meal has enough protein and carbs to keep you motivated.

Ingredients (2 servings):

300g smoked salmon

2 medium-sized ripe avocados, stoned and peeled

Juice from ½ lemon

handful tarragon leaves, chopped

2 slices of whole wheat bread, toasted

Prep time: 5 min

No cooking time

Preparation:

Cut the avocados into chunks and toss in the lemon juice. Twist and fold the smoked salmon pieces, place them on serving plates, then scatter with the avocado and tarragon. Serve with whole wheat toast.

Nutritional value per serving: 550kcal, 34g protein, 37g carbs (12g fiber, 4g sugar), 30g fat (5g saturated), 17% iron, 24% magnesium, 25% vitamin C, 27% vitamin E, 42% vitamin K, 16% vitamin B1, 24% vitamin B2, 55% vitamin B3, 35% vitamin B5, 40% vitamin B6, 35% vitamin B9, 81% vitamin B12.

13. Breakfast 'Pizza'

Forget about the high-calorie, non-nutritious slice of pizza and replace it with this delicious substitute. Healthy and filling, it only takes 20 min to make and it's not only high in protein, but also in minerals and vitamins.

Ingredients (1 serving):

1 small whole wheat pita

3 egg whites

1 egg

¼ cup low-fat mozzarella cheese

1 spring onion, sliced

¼ cup mushrooms, diced

¼ cup bell peppers, diced

2 slices turkey bacon, chopped

1 teaspoon olive oil

salt and pepper

Prep time: 10 min

Cooking time: 10 min

Preparation:

Whisk the eggs with a pinch of salt and pepper and add the diced vegetables.

Bend the edges of the pita bread to create a bowl. Brush both sides with the olive oil and place the pita bread on the grill, dome side down. Cook until golden then flip it on the other side.

Pour the egg mix into the pita and cook until the eggs are nearly done, add the turkey bacon, spring onion and cheese. Cook until the cheese had melted and serve.

Nutritional value per serving: 350kcal, 33g protein, 12g carbs (3g fiber, 4g sugar), 15g fat (6 saturated), 32% calcium, 19% iron, 15% magnesium, 36% vitamin A, 88% vitamin C, 72% vitamin K, 21% vitamin B1, 71% vitamin B2, 22% vitamin B3, 14% vitamin B5, 21% vitamin B6, 25% vitamin B9, 29% vitamin B12.

14. Mexican Mocha Breakfast

Top your favorite cup of oats with a healthy serving of almond milk and enjoy a quickly-made high-fiber breakfast. The cayenne pepper is perfect for adding a little oomph to your oatmeal.

Ingredients (1 serving):

½ cup rolled oats

1 scoop chocolate protein powder

½ tablespoon cinnamon

½ teaspoon cayenne pepper

1 cup unsweetened almond milk

1 tablespoon unsweetened cocoa powder

Prep time: 5 min

Cooking time: 3 min

Preparation:

Mix all the ingredients in a microwave-safe bowl. Heat in the microwave for 2 ½ -3 min then serve.

Nutritional value per serving: 304kcal, 27g protein, 38g carbs (8g fiber, 3g sugar), 7g fat, 32% calcium, 15% iron, 25% magnesium, 10% vitamin A, 25% vitamin D, 51% vitamin E, 12% vitamin B1.

15. Blueberry Lemon Pancakes

A warm, filling breakfast, this blueberry pancake enriched by the lemony flavor is a simple and tasty way of getting that high-powered meal that you need to start your day. Spread a tablespoon of Greek yogurt on top of your pancake if you like.

Ingredients (1 serving):

1/3 cup oat bran

5 egg whites

½ cup blueberries

1 scoop flavorless whey protein powder

½ teaspoon baking soda

1 teaspoon grated lemon peel

1 tablespoon lemon drink mix

olive oil spray

Prep time: 5 min

Cooking time: 5 min

Preparation:

Combine all the ingredients in a large bowl, mix and whisk until smooth.

Cook the batch in a sprayed skilled on medium-high temperature until bubbles form on the surface. Flip over and cook until each side is dark golden brown. Remove the pancake and serve.

Nutritional value per serving: 340kcal, 47g protein, 37g carbs (6g fiber, 14g sugar), 5g fat, 10% iron, 25% magnesium, 12% vitamin C, 19% vitamin K, 26% vitamin B1, 58% vitamin B2.

LUNCH

16. Mediterranean Rice

Turn the tired can of tuna into a delicious dish that is a perfect starter for an afternoon of exercise. The high amount of carbs will fuel a thorough workout and the protein will make sure that your muscles recuperate from the effort.

Ingredients (1 serving):

1 can of tuna in oil, drained

100g brown rice

¼ avocado, chopped

¼ red onion, sliced

juice from ½ lemon

salt and pepper

Prep time: 5 min

Cooking time: 20 min

Preparation:

Boil the brown rice for approximately 20 min then place in a bowl with the onion, tuna and avocado. Add the lemon juice and mix all the ingredients. Season with salt and pepper to taste and serve.

Nutritional value per serving: 590kcal, 32g protein, 80g carbs (7g fiber, 1g sugar), 14g fat (5g saturated), 22% iron, 52% magnesium, 101% vitamin D, 18% vitamin E, 107% vitamin K, 32% vitamin B1, 134% vitamin B3, 26% vitamin B5, 39% vitamin B6, 15% vitamin B9, 63% vitamin B12.

17. Spiced Chicken

Chicken is perfect for a high protein muscle building meal. High in nutrients across the board, this simple, tasty meal can be paired with a serving of your choice of carbs.

Ingredients (2 servings):

3 boneless chicken breasts cut in half

175g low-fat yogurt

5cm piece cucumber, finely chopped

2 tablespoons Thai red curry paste

2 tablespoons cilantro, chopped

2 cups raw spinach, to serve.

Prep time: 5 min

Cooking time: 35-40 min

Preparation:

Preheat the oven to 190C fan/ gas 5. Put the chicken in a dish in one layer. Blend a third of the yogurt, the curry paste and two thirds of the cilantro, add salt and pour over the chicken, making sure the meat is evenly coated. Leave for 30 min (or in the fridge overnight).

Lift the chicken onto a rack in a roasting tin for 35-40 min, until golden.

Heat water in a pan and wilt the spinach.

Mix the rest of the yogurt and cilantro, add the cucumber and stir. Pour the mix over the chicken and serve with the cooked spinach.

Nutritional value per serving: 275kcal, 43g protein, 8g carbs (1g fiber, 8g sugar), 3g fat (1g saturated), 20% calcium, 15% iron, 25% magnesium, 56% vitamin A, 18% vitamin C, 181% vitamin K, 16% vitamin B1, 26% vitamin B2, 133% vitamin B3, 25% vitamin B5, 67% vitamin B6, 19% vitamin B9, 22% vitamin B12.

18. Stuffed Eggs with Pita Bread

Get your fill of omega-3 fatty acids with this rich salmon dish. High in vitamins and minerals, this filling meal is a great way of boosting yourself with energy and powering through your day.

Ingredients (2 servings):

1 canned salmon in water (450g)

2 eggs

1 large spring onions, finely chopped

2 large leafs of lettuce

10 cherry tomatoes

1 tablespoon Greek yogurt

a large whole wheat pita bread, cut in half

sea salt and pepper

Prep time: 10 min

Cooking time: 10 min

Preparation:

Boil the eggs, peel them and slice them in half then remove the yolks and place them in a bowl.

Add the canned salmon, 1 tablespoon of yogurt, the spring onion and the seasonings to the bowl. Mix all the ingredients together and stuff the egg whites. Serve with pita bread stuffed with lettuce and tomatoes.

Nutritional value per serving: 455kcal, 45g protein, 24g carbs (3g fiber, 2g sugar), 36g fat (10g saturated), 59% calcium, 22% iron, 21% magnesium, 30% vitamin A, 24% vitamin C, 43% vitamin K, 11% vitamin B1, 36% vitamin B2, 60% vitamin B3, 20% vitamin B5, 41% vitamin B6, 20% vitamin B9, 20% vitamin B12.

19. Chicken Caesar Wraps

These chicken wraps make a great portable meal that will make sure that you keep your protein levels high throughout the day. Throw in some baby spinach and make a more green friendly meal.

Ingredients (1 serving):

85g chicken breast, baked

2 whole wheat tortillas

1 cup lettuce

50g non-fat yogurt

1 teaspoon anchovy paste

1 teaspoon dry mustard powder

1 clove garlic, cooked

½ medium cucumber, chopped

Prep time: 5 min

No cooking

Preparation:

Combine the anchovy paste, garlic and yogurt then toss and coat the lettuce and cucumbers. Split the mix in 2, add to the tortillas and then place half the chicken in each tortilla. Wrap up and serve.

Nutritional value per serving (2 tortillas): 460kcal, 41g protein, 57g carbs (7g fiber, 9g sugar), 10g fat (2g saturated), 11% calcium, 22% vitamin K, 13% vitamin B2, 59% vitamin B3, 12% vitamin B5, 29% vitamin B6, 10% vitamin B12.

20. Baked Salmon with Grilled Asparagus

A classic dish, made more interesting by a marinade of lemon juice and mustard, this grilled salmon goes well with the garlicky asparagus spears. Treat yourself to a great combination of protein and vitamins.

Ingredients (1 serving):

140g wild salmon

1 ½ cup asparagus

Marinade:

1 tablespoon garlic, minced

1 tablespoon Dijon mustard

lemon juice from ½ lemon

1 teaspoon olive oil

Prep time: 5 min

Cooking time: 15 min

Preparation:

Preheat oven to 200C fan/ gas 6.

In a bowl, mix the lemon juice, half the garlic, olive oil and mustard, pour the marinade over the salmon and make sure it is completely covered. Place the marinating salmon in the fridge for at least one hour.

Cut the bottom stems off the asparagus spears. Set a nonstick skillet on medium/high heat, toss the asparagus with the remaining garlic and sear for about 5 min, rolling the asparagus on all sides.

Place the salmon on a baking sheet and bake for 10 min then serve with the grilled asparagus.

Nutritional value: 350kcal, 43g protein, 7g carbs (5g fiber, 1 g sugar), 16g fat (1 saturated), 17% iron, 20% magnesium, 48% vitamin A, 119% vitamin C, 17% vitamin E, 288% vitamin K, 39% vitamin B1, 60% vitamin B2, 90% vitamin B3, 33% vitamin B5, 74% vitamin B6, 109% vitamin B9, 75% vitamin B12.

21. Beef Meatball Pasta with Spinach

A high-protein pasta meal that makes the most of the beef and spinach pairing. Not only is it all-round vitamin packed, but it also contains a hearty amount of magnesium which helps regulate muscle contraction.

Ingredients (2 servings):

For meatballs:

170g lean ground beef

½ cup raw spinach, shredded

1 tablespoon minced garlic

¼ cup red onion, diced

1 teaspoon cumin

sea salt and pepper

For Pasta:

100g wheat spinach pasta

10 cherry tomatoes

2 cups raw spinach

¼ cup marinara

2 tablespoons low-fat parmesan cheese

Prep time: 15 min

Cooking time: 30 min

Preparation:

Preheat oven to 200C/ gas 6.

Mix together the ground beef, raw spinach, garlic, red onion and salt and pepper to taste. Mix thoroughly with your hands until the spinach is completely mixed into the meat.

Form two or three meatballs, roughly the same size then place them on a baking sheet in the oven for 10-12 minutes.

Cook the pasta according to the instructions on the pack. Drain the pasta and stir in the tomatoes, spinach and cheese. Add the meatballs and serve.

Nutritional value per serving: 470kcal, 33g protein, 50g carbs (6g fiber, 5g sugar), 12g fat (5g saturated), 17% calcium, 28% iron, 74% magnesium, 104% vitamin A, 38% vitamin C, 11% vitamin E, 361% vitamin K, 16% vitamin B1,

20% vitamin B2, 45% vitamin B3, 11% vitamin B5, 45% vitamin B6, 35% vitamin B9, 37% vitamin B12.

22. Stuffed Chicken Breast with Brown Rice

Brown rice is an excellent way of introducing quality carbs to your diet. Couple it with high-protein chicken breast and some vegetables and you have a delicious power lunch.

Ingredients (1 serving):

170g chicken breast

½ cup raw spinach

50g brown rice

1 spring onion, diced

1 tomato, sliced

1 tablespoon feta cheese

Prep time: 10 min

Cooking time: 30 min

Preparation:

Preheat the oven to 190C fan/ gas 5.

Slice the chicken breast down the middle to make it look like a butterfly. Season the chicken with salt and pepper, then open it and layer spinach, feta cheese and tomato slices on one side. Fold the chicken breast and use a toothpick to hold it closed then bake for 20 min.

Boil the brown rice then add the garlic and chopped onion. Fill a plate with brown rice, place the chicken on top and serve.

Nutritional value per serving: 469kcal, 48g protein, 46g carbs (5g fiber, 6g sugar), 8g fat (5g saturated), 22% calcium, 18% iron, 38% magnesium, 55% vitamin A, 43% vitamin C, 169% vitamin K, 28% vitamin B1, 28% vitamin B2, 103% vitamin B3, 28% vitamin B5, 70% vitamin B6, 23% vitamin B9, 17% vitamin B12.

23. Shrimp and Zucchini Linguine Pasta Salad

A cheat pasta meal with a serving of shredded zucchini and steamed shrimp flavored with all manners of sesame. This combination of ingredients makes for a light lunch with a high-protein content.

Ingredients (1 serving):

170g steamed shrimp

1 large zucchini, chopped

¼ cup red onion, sliced

1 cup bell peppers, sliced

1 tablespoon roasted Tahini butter

1 teaspoon sesame oil

1 teaspoon sesame seeds

Prep time: 10 min

No cooking

Preparation:

Cut the zucchini using a shredder in order to make raw linguine.

In a bowl, mix tahini and sesame oil.

Place all the ingredients in a large bowl, pour the Tahini sauce and toss it to make sure all sides are covered in sauce. Sprinkle some sesame seeds and serve.

Nutritional value per serving: 420kcal, 45g protein, 26g carbs (10g fiber, 12g sugar), 18g fat (2g saturated), 19% calcium, 47% iron, 48% magnesium, 33% vitamin A, 303% vitamin C, 17% vitamin E, 31% vitamin K, 38% vitamin B1, 36% vitamin B2, 38% vitamin B3, 13% vitamin B5, 66% vitamin B6, 35% vitamin B9, 42% vitamin B12.

24. Turkey Meatloaf with Whole Wheat Couscous

Cooked in a muffin pan, this turkey meatloaf makes sure that you minimize you saturated fats intake. Mix it up a little by adding bell pepper or mushrooms instead of onion into the meatballs and by seasoning with a pinch of ground garlic.

Ingredients (1 serving):

140g lean ground turkey

¾ cup red onions, diced

1 cup raw spinach

1/3 cup low sodium marinara sauce

½ cup whole wheat couscous, boiled

choice of seasoning: Parsley, Basil, Coriander

pepper, salt

olive oil spray

Prep time: 5 min

Cooking time: 20 min

Preparation:

Preheat oven to 200C fan/ gas 6.

Season turkey with your choice of seasoning and add the diced onions.

Light spray your muffin pan with olive oil, place the ground turkey inside the muffin holders. Top each turkey meatball with 1 tablespoon marinara sauce, then place in the oven and bake for 8-10 min.

Serve with couscous.

Nutritional value per serving: 460kcal, 34g protein, 53g carbs (4g fiber, 7g sugar), 12g fat (4g saturated), 12% calcium, 15% iron, 10% magnesium, 16% vitamin A, 15% vitamin C, 11% vitamin E, 16% vitamin K, 11% vitamin B1, 25% vitamin B3, 16% vitamin B6, 11% vitamin B9.

25. Tuna Burger and Salad

The tuna burger is high in protein and carbs, making it an excellent choice for a workout day meal. Fix it differently every time and keep it interesting by switching between vegetables and seasoning your salad dressing.

Ingredients (1 serving):

1 canned chunk tuna (165g)

1 egg white

½ cup chopped mushrooms

2 cups lettuce, shredded

¼ cup dried oats

1 teaspoon olive oil

1 tablespoons low-fat salad dressing (of preference)

small bunch of oregano, chopped

1 whole wheat medium roll cut in half

Prep time: 10 min

Cooking time: 10 min

Preparation:

Mix together the egg white, tuna, dry oats, oregano and form a patty.

Heat the oil in a non-stick pan on medium heat, place the patty on and flip it to make sure it cooks on both sides.

Cut the whole wheat roll in half, horizontally, place the patty between the 2 pieces.

Mix the vegetables in a bowl, add the salad dressing and serve next to the tuna burger.

Nutritional value per serving: 560kcal, 52g protein, 76g carbs (13g fiber, 7g sugar), 10g fat (1g saturated), 11% calcium, 35% iron, 38% magnesium, 16% vitamin A, 16% vitamin K, 35% vitamin B1, 33% vitamin B2, 24% vitamin B3, 28% vitamin B5, 41% vitamin B6, 21% vitamin B9, 82% vitamin B12.

26. Spicy Beefsteak Kebabs

This spicy kebab is served with a side of baked potato, making it not only a muscle building meal but also a great way of introducing eyesight protecting vitamin A to your diet. Add a tablespoon of low-fat yogurt to your potato to make it more refreshing.

Ingredients (1 serving):

140g lean beef flank steak

200g sweet potato

1 bell pepper, chopped

½ medium zucchini, chopped

minced garlic

pepper, salt

Prep time: 15 min

Cooking time: 55 min

Preparation:

Preheat oven to 200C fan/ gas 6. Wrap the sweet potato in a foil, place in the oven and bake for 45 min.

Cut the flank steak into small pieces, season with salt, pepper and garlic. Assemble the kebab, alternating between beef, zucchini and bell pepper.

Place the kebab on a baking sheet and bake for 10 min. Serve with the sweet potato.

Nutritional value per serving: 375kcal, 38g protein, 49g carbs (9g fiber, 12g sugar), 4g fat (1g saturated), 24% iron, 27% magnesium, 581% vitamin A, 195% vitamin C, 21% vitamin K, 22% vitamin B1, 28% vitamin B2, 61% vitamin B3, 28% vitamin B5, 92% vitamin B6, 20% vitamin B9, 30% vitamin B12.

27. Trout with Potatoes Salad

Want to make sure that you are not lacking in vitamin B12? Try this hearty portion of trout, paired with a nutrient and vitamin packed fresh-tasting potato salad.

Ingredients (2 servings):

2*140g trout fillets

250g waxy potatoes, halved

4 teaspoons yogurt

4 teaspoons reduced-fat mayonnaise

1 tablespoon capers, rinsed

4 small cornichons, sliced

2 spring onions, finely sliced

¼ cucumber, diced

1 lemon, zest from ½

Prep time: 10 min

Cooking time: 20 min

Preparation:

Boil the potatoes in salted water for 15 min until they are just tender. Drain and rinse under cold water, then drain again.

Heat the grill.

Mix the mayonnaise and yogurt and season with some lemon juice. Stir the mix into the potatoes with the capers, most of the spring onion, cucumber and cornichons. Scatter the salad with the rest of the onions.

Season the trout, grill on a baking sheet, skin-side down, until just cooked. Scatter with the lemon zest and serve with the potato salad.

Nutritional value per serving: 420kcal, 38g protein, 28g carbs (3g fiber, 6g sugar), 13g fat (3g saturated), 12% calcium, 11% iron, 22% magnesium, 29% vitamin C, 59% vitamin K, 21% vitamin B1, 18% vitamin B2, 12% vitamin B3, 22% vitamin B5, 43% vitamin B6, 18% vitamin B9, 153% vitamin B12.

28. Mexican Bean Chili

A high in protein midday meal, this dish is a great way of getting 1/3 of your daily required amount of fiber. Though it has enough nutrients to be a stand-alone meal, it can also be served on top of a bed of brown rice.

Ingredients (2 servings):

250g minced beef

200g caned baked beans

75ml beef stock

½ onion, diced

½ red pepper, diced

1 teaspoon chipotle paste

1 teaspoon olive oil

½ teaspoon chili powder

1 cup brown rice, boiled (optional)

coriander leaves, o serve

Prep time: 5 min

Cooking time: 45 min

Preparation:

Heat the oil in a non-stick pan over medium heat then fry the onion and red pepper until softened. Increase the heat, add the chili powder and cook for 2 min before adding the minced beef. Cook until browned and all the liquid has evaporated.

Tip in the beef stock, baked beans and chipotle paste. Simmer over a low heat for 20 min, then season and scatter with coriander leaves and serve with the boiled rice.

Nutritional value per serving (without rice): 402kcal, 34g protein, 19g carbs (5g fiber, 10g sugar), 14g fat (5g saturated), 29% iron, 15% magnesium, 42% vitamin C, 11% vitamin B1, 16% vitamin B2, 34% vitamin B3, 40% vitamin B6, 18% vitamin B9, 52% vitamin B12.

½ cup of rice: 108kcal

29. Beef and Broccoli Noodles

A convenient, tasty dish, the beef and broccoli noodles take only 20 min to prepare, making it a great choice for a busy day. You can serve with a few slices of red chili for some extra spice.

Ingredients (2 servings):

2 cups egg noodles

200g beef stir-fry strips

1 spring onion, sliced

½ head broccoli, small florets

1 teaspoon sesame oil

For the sauce:

1 ½ tablespoons low-salt soy sauce

1 teaspoon tomato ketchup

1 garlic clove, crushed

1 tablespoon oyster sauce

¼ knob ginger, finely grated

1 teaspoon white wine vinegar

Prep time: 10 min

Cooking time: 10 min

Preparation:

Mix the ingredients for the sauce. Boil the noodles according to the pack instructions. Tip in the broccoli when they are almost ready. Leave for a few minutes then drain the noodles and broccoli.

Heat the oil in a wok until very hot then stir-fry the beef for 2-3 minutes until browned. Tip the sauce, stir, and let it simmer for a few moments then turn off the heat.

Stir the beef into the noodles, scatter with the spring onion and serve immediately.

Nutritional value per serving: 352kcal, 33g protein, 39g carbs (5g fiber, 5g sugar), 9g fat (2g saturated), 20% iron, 20% magnesium, 20% vitamin A, 224% vitamin C, 214% vitamin K, 14% vitamin B1, 19% vitamin B2, 43% vitamin B3, 18% vitamin B5, 50% vitamin B6, 31% vitamin B9, 23% vitamin B12.

30. Pancetta-wrapped Pollock with Potatoes

This light and fresh-tasting dish provides a lot of energy and is high in protein, making it an ideal option for a midday meal. The pollock can be substituted for another sustainable white fish, while the olives can be replaced by sundried tomatoes.

Ingredients (2 servings):

2* 140g pollock fillets

4 slices pancetta

300g new potatoes

100g green beans

30g kalamata olives

juice and zest from 1 lemon

2 tablespoons olive oil

a few tarragon sprigs, leaves picked

Prep time: 10 min

Cooking time 15 min

Preparation:

Heat oven to 200C fan/ gas 6. Boil the potatoes for 10-12 min until tender, add the beans for the final 2-3 min. Drain well, slice the potatoes in half and tip into a baking dish. Toss with the olives, lemon zest and oil and season well.

Season the fish and wrap with the pancetta then place it on top of the potatoes. Bake for 10-12 min until cooked through, then add the lemon juice, scatter with tarragon and serve.

Nutritional value per serving: 525kcal, 46g protein, 36g carbs (5g fiber, 3g sugar), 31g fat (8g saturated), 10% iron, 31% magnesium, 63% vitamin C, 18% vitamin K, 15% vitamin B1, 13% vitamin B2, 14% vitamin B3, 25% vitamin B6, 73% vitamin B12.

DINNER

31. Sushi Bowl

A low-calorie sushi bowl that substitutes rice for cauliflower flavored with garlic, soy sauce and lime juice for extra taste. Use the seaweed sheets to wrap the veggies and salmon and make a mini roll.

Ingredients (2 servings):

170g smoked salmon

1 medium-sized avocado

½ head cauliflower, steamed and chopped

1/3 cup carrot, shredded

½ teaspoon cayenne

1.2 teaspoon garlic powder

1 tablespoon low-sodium soy sauce

2 seaweed sheets

Juice from ½ lime

Prep time: 10 min

No cooking

Preparation:

Place the cauliflower, carrots, soy sauce, garlic, lime juice and cayenne in a food processor. Stop blending before the mix turns into a paste. Serve next to the salmon and seaweed sheets.

Nutritional value per serving: 272kcal, 20g protein, 13g carbs (7g fiber, 4g sugar), 16g fat (1g saturated), 10% iron, 14% magnesium, 73% vitamin A, 88% vitamin C, 13% vitamin E, 40% vitamin K, 18% vitamin B1, 15% vitamin B2, 31% vitamin B3, 21% vitamin B5, 31% vitamin B6, 26% vitamin B9, 45% vitamin B12.

32. Sweet and Sour Chicken

The sweet and sour chicken is a simple, delicious recipe that has a place in every fit kitchen. It is high in protein and vitamins and goes well with steamed broccoli florets.

Ingredients (2 servings):

300g chicken breasts cut into bite-sized pieces

1 teaspoon garlic salt

¼ cup low sodium chicken broth

¼ cup white vinegar

¼ no-calorie sweetener

¼ teaspoon black pepper

1 teaspoon low-sodium soy sauce

3 teaspoons low-sugar ketchup

arrowroot

400g broccoli florets, steamed

Prep time: 10 min

Cooking time 15 min

Preparation:

Place the chicken in a large bowl and season with the garlic, pepper and salt, turning to coat. Cook the chicken over medium/high heat until done.

In the meantime, whisk together the chicken broth, sweetener, vinegar, ketchup and soy sauce in a sauce pan, bring the mix to a boil and turn to low heat. Add the arrowroot a little at a time and whisk briskly. Keep stirring for a few minutes.

Pour sauce over the cooked chicken and serve with a side of steamed broccoli.

Nutritional value per serving: 250kcal, 40g protein, 14g carbs (6g fiber, 4g sugar), 2g fat, 11% calcium, 14% iron, 20% magnesium, 24% vitamin A, 303% vitamin C, 254% vitamin K, 17% vitamin B1, 21% vitamin B2, 90% vitamin B3, 24% vitamin B5, 58% vitamin B6, 33% vitamin B9.

33. Garlicky Hummus

You only need 5 min to make this healthy, delicious meal. It is chock-full with magnesium and has a decent amount of protein considering the recipe is meatless. Grab a whole wheat tortilla and make this meal to go.

Ingredients (3 servings):

1*400g canned chickpeas (save 1/4 of the liquid)

¼ cup tahini

¼ cup lemon juice

1 clove garlic

1 tablespoon olive oil

¼ teaspoon ground ginger

¼ teaspoon ground cumin

2 spring onions, finely chopped

1 tomato, chopped

Prep time: 5 min

No cooking

Preparation:

Place the chickpeas, liquid, tahini, lemon juice, olive oil, garlic, cumin and ginger in a food processor and blend until smooth.

Stir in the tomato and scallions and season with salt and pepper. Serve next to slices of bell pepper.

Nutritional value per serving: 324kcal, 11g protein, 21g carbs (7g fiber, 1g sugar), 17g fat (2g saturated), 22% calcium, 54% iron, 135% magnesium, 10% vitamin A, 12% vitamin C, 33% vitamin K, 122% vitamin B1, 12% vitamin B2, 44% vitamin B3, 11% vitamin B5, 12% vitamin B6, 40% vitamin B9.

34. Chicken with Pineapple and Bell Peppers

Take a break from the usual chicken recipes and try this version with sweet, fresh pineapple. High in vitamin B3 and protein, this meal is also an important source of carbs. In tone with the change of pace, you can substitute the rice for quinoa.

Ingredients (1 serving):

140g boneless chicken breast,

1 tablespoon mustard

½ cup fresh pineapple, diced

½ cup bell peppers, diced

50g brown rice

Coconut oil spray

1 teaspoon cumin

salt and pepper

Prep time: 5 min

Cooking time: 15 min

Preparation:

Cut the chicken into small pieces then rub the mustard on the pieces and season with salt, pepper and cumin.

Set a skillet on medium heat and lightly spray with coconut oil, add the chicken and cook on all sides. When the chicken is almost finished, increase the heat and toss in the pineapple pieces and bell peppers, cook and make sure that all sides are brown. This should take 3-5 min.

Boil the brown rice and serve next to the chicken.

Nutritional value per serving: 377kcal, 37g protein, 50g carbs (6g fiber, 10g sugar), 1g fat, 12% iron, 33% magnesium, 168% vitamin C, 26% vitamin B1, 13% vitamin B2, 96% vitamin B3, 22% vitamin B5, 65% vitamin B6, 10% vitamin B9.

35. Mexican Style Protein Bowl

Give yourself a break from meat and throw these ingredients together for a tasty alternative to the usual. You can skip the fried fat and unhealthy calories and still get the flavor of a Mexican meal.

Ingredients:

1/3 cup cooked black beans

½ cup cooked brown rice

2 tablespoons salsa

¼ avocado, sliced

Prep time: 5 min

No cooking

Preparation:

Combine all the ingredients in a bowl and serve.

Nutritional value per serving: 307kcal, 11g protein, 48g carbs (11g fiber, 1g sugar), 7g fat (1g sugar), 26%

magnesium, 13% vitamin K, 16% vitamin B1, 11% vitamin B3, 17% vitamin B6, 30% vitamin B9.

36. Arugula Chicken Salad

The arugula leaves add satisfaction to this sweet and super healthy salad. Bountiful in vegetables and quality protein source, this meal can be enriched with a simple dressing of low-fat yogurt and garlic.

Ingredients (1 serving):

120g chicken breast

5 baby carrots, chopped

¼ red cabbage, chopped

½ cup arugula

1 tablespoon sunflower seeds

1 teaspoon olive oil

Prep time: 10 min

Cooking time: 10 min

Preparation:

Cut the chicken into bite-sized cubes. Heat the olive oil in a non-stick pan and fry the chicken until it is cooked. Set aside and allow cooling.

Place the carrots, arugula and cabbage in a large bowl. Top the salad with the cooled chicken and sunflower seeds and serve.

Nutritional value per serving: 311kcal, 30g protein, 9g carbs (1g fiber), 13g fat (1g saturated), 11% iron, 22% magnesium, 150% vitamin A, 25% vitamin C, 29% vitamin E, 32% vitamin K, 23% vitamin B1, 10% vitamin B2, 72% vitamin B3, 11% vitamin B5, 49% vitamin B6, 17% vitamin B9.

37. Dijon Mustard Halibut

This tangy halibut meal is a fast-and-easy way to get a hearty dose of protein. It's low in carbs and high in vitamins, making it a perfect choice for supper. The low calorie count allows you to double the sauce if you are feeling indulgent.

Ingredients (2 servings):

220g halibut

¼ onion, diced

1 red pepper, diced

1 clove garlic

1 tablespoon Dijon mustard

1 teaspoon Worcestershire sauce

1 teaspoon olive oil

juice from 1 lemon

a bunch of parsley

2 large carrots cut into sticks

1 cup broccoli florets

1 cup mushrooms, sliced

Prep time: 10 min

Cooking time: 20 min

Preparation:

Place the red pepper, garlic, parsley, mustard, onion Worcestershire sauce, lemon juice and olive oil in a food processor.

Place the fish, sauce and the rest of the vegetables in a large parchment baking bag. Bake at 190C fan/ gas 5 for 20 min then serve.

Nutritional value per serving: 225kcal, 33g protein, 12g carbs (3g fiber, 5g sugar), 5g fat (1g saturated), 11% calcium, 10% iron, 35% magnesium, 180% vitamin A, 77% vitamin C, 71% vitamin K, 13% vitamin B1, 19% vitamin B2, 51% vitamin B3, 14% vitamin B5, 34% vitamin B6, 15% vitamin B9, 25% vitamin B12.

38. Tray Bake Chicken

Quick, easy and tasty, this dish should be a summer staple in your kitchen since there is no shortage of fresh cherry tomatoes. The pesto adds a refreshing flavor to a simply seasoned chicken breast.

Ingredients (2 servings):

300g chicken breast

300g cherry tomatoes

2 tablespoons pesto

1 tablespoon olive oil

salt, pepper

Prep time: 5 min

Cooking time: 15 min

Preparation:

Place the chicken breast in a roasting tray, season, drizzle with the olive oil then grill for 10 min. Add the cherry tomatoes and grill for another 5 min until the chicken is cooked. Spread pesto over the top and serve next to the cherry tomatoes.

Nutritional value per serving: 312kcal, 36g protein, 7g carbs (2g fiber, 5g sugar), 19g fat (4g saturated), 15% magnesium, 25% vitamin A, 34% vitamin C, 11% vitamin E, 20% vitamin K, 10% vitamin B1, 88% vitamin B3, 13% vitamin B5, 33% vitamin B6.

39. Tofu burger

Tofu has all of the essential amino acids, and that makes it a perfect substitute for meat. The caramelized onions with chili flakes and Sriracha, paired with the teriyaki infused tofu will delight your taste buds.

Ingredients (1 serving):

85g tofu (extra firm)

1 tablespoon teriyaki marinade

1 tablespoon Sriracha

1 lettuce leaf

30g carrot, shredded

¼ red onion, sliced

½ teaspoon red chili flakes

1 medium-sized whole wheat roll

Prep time: 5 min

Cooking time: 10 min

Preparation:

Heat the grill.

Marinate the tofu in teriyaki marinade, red chili flakes and Sriracha then grill it for 3-5 min on each side.

Fry the red onion in a non-stick pan until caramelized.

Cut the roll in half until you can open it like a book. Stuff the roll with the grilled tofu, caramelized onion, carrots and lettuce and serve.

Nutritional value per serving: 194kcal, 11g protein, 28g carbs (5g fiber, 8g sugar), 5g fat (1g saturated), 21% calcium, 14% iron, 19% magnesium, 95% vitamin A, 10% vitamin B1, 14% vitamin B6.

40. Hot Cod

High in protein and healthy fats and low in carbs, this super spicy cod will give a jolt for the rest of your day. Serve it with a bit of brown rice if you need a carb boost for an evening workout and add 2 more peppers if you feel you can handle more spice.

Ingredients (2 servings):

340g white cod

10 cherry tomatoes, halved

2 jalapeno peppers, sliced

2 tablespoons olive oil

sea salt

chili powder

Prep time: 5 min

Cooking time: 10 min

Preparation:

Heat the oil in a non-stick pan. Coat the cod in salt and chili powder, add to the pan and cook for 10 min on medium heat. Toss in the peppers 1-2 min before the fish is cooked through.

Serve with cherry tomatoes.

Nutritional value per serving: 279kcal, 30g protein, 6g carbs (1g fiber, 1 g sugar), 16g fat (2g saturated), 11% magnesium, 17% vitamin A, 38% vitamin C, 26% vitamin E, 33% vitamin K, 24% vitamin B3, 43% vitamin B6, 26% vitamin B12.

41. Grilled Mushroom and Zucchini Burger

The Portobello mushrooms have a thick, meaty texture that makes them a favorite among vegetarians and meat lovers alike. Indulge in nature's burger and get a load of minerals and vitamins at a minimal calorie cost.

Ingredients (1 serving):

1 large portabella mushroom cap

¼ small zucchini, sliced

1 teaspoon roasted bell peppers

1 slice of low fat cheese

4 spinach leaves

olive oil spray

1 medium-sized whole wheat roll

Prep time: 5 min

Cooking time: 5 min

Preparation:

Heat the grill. Spray the mushroom cap with olive oil then grill both mushroom and zucchini slices.

Cut the roll in half, horizontally, then place the ingredients in layers on one half and cover with the other. Serve immediately.

Nutritional value per serving: 185kcal, 12g protein, 24g carbs (4g fiber, 5g sugar), 4g fat (1g saturated), 21% calcium, 17% iron, 20% magnesium, 78% vitamin A, 28% vitamin C, 242% vitamin K, 15% vitamin B1, 37% vitamin B2, 26% vitamin B3, 16% vitamin B5, 16% vitamin B6, 31% vitamin B9.

42. Mediterranean Fish

What better way to reach your daily B12 requirement than with a dish bursting of Mediterranean flavors? The rest of the vitamins and minerals are also well represented and the protein count is at a good amount for a light supper.

Ingredients (2 servings):

200g fresh trout

2 medium-sized tomatoes

3 teaspoons capers

½ red bell pepper, chopped

1 garlic clove, chopped

10 green olives, sliced

¼ onion, chopped

½ cup spinach

1 tablespoon olive oil

salt and pepper

Prep time: 10 min

Cooking time: 15 min

Preparation:

Heat a large pan over medium heat; add whole tomatoes, garlic and olive oil. Cover and let it simmer for a few minutes until the tomatoes begin to soften.

Add the onion, bell pepper, olives, capers, salt and pepper (and a little water if necessary). Cover and let it simmer until the tomatoes have broken down and the bell pepper and onion have softened.

Add the trout, cover and poach for 5-7 min.

Add the spinach at the last minute then serve.

Nutritional value per serving: 305kcal, 24g protein, 7g carbs (1g fiber, 4g sugar), 11g fat (3g saturated), 10% calcium, 12% magnesium, 36% vitamin A, 56% vitamin C, 62% vitamin K, 13% vitamin B1, 33% vitamin B3, 12% vitamin B5, 25% vitamin B6, 15% vitamin B9, 105% vitamin B12.

43. Vegan friendly dinner

A vegan friendly meal with a good amount of protein and vitamins. Give your palate the taste it deserves with this sweet and spicy sauce that flavors a filling amount of tofu and is easy to make.

Ingredients (2 servings):

340g tofu

¼ cup soy sauce

¼ cup brown sugar

2 teaspoons sesame oil

1 teaspoon olive oil

1 teaspoon chili flakes

2 garlic cloves, minced

1 teaspoon ginger, freshly grated

salt

Prep time: 5 min

Cooking time: 15 min

Preparation:

Mix the brown sugar, soy sauce, sesame oil, ginger, chili flakes and salt in a bowl and set aside.

Pour olive oil into a sauce pan and heat then fry the tofu for about 10 min.

Pour the sauce into the pan and cook for 3-5 min. Serve when the sauce has thickened and the tofu is done.

Nutritional value per serving: 245kcal, 17g protein, 15g carbs (1g fiber, 11g sugar), 15g fat (3g saturated), 34% calcium, 19% iron, 19% magnesium, 11% vitamin B2, 11% vitamin B6.

44. Tuna Melt

Unlike a regular tuna melt that is high in saturated fats and carbs, this one has a moderate amount of carbs and packs the protein-punch of a tuna can, making it an excellent meal that supports lean muscle growth.

Ingredients (2 servings):

1 can of tuna (165g)

2 slices of low-fat mozzarella cheese

2 teaspoons tomato sauce

1 whole wheat English muffin

a sprinkle of oregano

Prep time: 5 min

Cooking time: 3 min

Preparation:

Preheat the oven to 190C fan/ gas 5.

Slice the English muffin then smear each half with the tomato sauce. Top with the tuna, sprinkle with the oregano and place one slice of cheese on top of the tuna. Place the mini-melts in the oven and bake for 2-3 min or until the cheese has melted then divide between 2 plates and serve.

Nutritional value per serving: 255kcal, 31g protein, 14g carbs (2g fiber, 2 g sugar), 6g fat (4g saturated), 29% calcium, 11% iron, 13% magnesium, 10% vitamin B1, 10% vitamin B2, 60% vitamin B3, 23% vitamin B6, 52% vitamin B12.

45. Chicken with Avocado Salad

A meal that provides a great balance of quality protein and healthy fats that will keep you satisfied without overdoing it on the carbs front. Replace the vinegar with lemon juice for a fresher feel.

Ingredients (1 serving):

100g chicken breast

1 teaspoon smoked paprika

2 teaspoons olive oil

For the salad:

½ medium avocado, diced

1 medium tomato, chopped

½ small red onion, thinly sliced

1 tablespoon parsley, roughly chopped

1 teaspoon red wine vinegar

Prep time: 10 min

Cooking time: 10 min

Preparation:

Heat the grill to medium. Rub the chicken with 1 teaspoon olive oil and paprika. Cook for 5 min on each side until it is cooked through and lightly charred. Cut the chicken in thick slices.

Mix the salad ingredients together, season, add the rest of the olive oil and serve with the chicken.

Nutritional value per serving: 346kcal, 26g protein, 14g carbs (6g fiber, 4g sugar), 22g fat (3g saturated), 16% magnesium, 22% vitamin, 44% vitamin C, 18% vitamin E, 38% vitamin K, 12% vitamin B1, 11% vitamin B2, 66% vitamin B3, 19% vitamin B5, 43% vitamin B6, 22% vitamin B9.

SNACKS

1. Cherry Tomatoes with Cottage Cheese

Cut 5 cherry tomatoes in half and smear them with 2 tablespoons goat cheese mixed with fresh dill and a pinch of salt.

Nutritional value: 58kcal, 4g protein, 10g carbs, 30% vitamin A, 40% vitamin C, 20% vitamin K, 10% vitamin B1, 10% vitamin B6, 10% vitamin B9.

2. Avocado on Toast

Toast a small piece of whole wheat bread then cover it with 50g of mashed avocado and sprinkle with salt and pepper.

Nutritional value: 208kcal, 5g protein, 28g carbs (6g fiber, 2g sugar), 9g fat (1g saturated), 13% vitamin K, 13% vitamin B9.

3. Bell Peppers with Cottage Cheese

Cut a small bell pepper in half, deseed it then stuff it with 50g cottage cheese mixed with your choice of seasoning.

Nutritional value: 44kcal, 6g protein, 3g carbs (3g sugar), 49% vitamin C.

4. Rice Cake with Peanut Butter

Spread 1 rice cake with 1 tablespoon creamy peanut butter.

Nutritional value: 129kcal, 5g protein, 10g carbs (1g fiber, 1 g sugar), 8g fat (1g saturated), 10% vitamin B3.

5. Celery Sticks with Goat Cheese and Green Olives

Top 3 medium celery sticks with 3 tablespoons goat cheese and 3 sliced green olives.

Nutritional value: 102kcal, 4g protein, 6g carbs (3g fiber), 6g fat (4g saturated), 12% calcium, 45% vitamin K, 18% vitamin A, 12% vitamin B9.

6. Yogurt with Dried Goji Berries

Mix 150g low-fat yogurt with 10g goji berries.

Nutritional value: 134kcal, 7g protein, 19g carbs (1g fiber, 18% sugar), 4g fat (1g saturated), 27% calcium, 24% iron, 13% vitamin C, 19% vitamin B2, 13% vitamin B12.

7. Apple and Peanut Butter

Slice 1 small apple and spread 1 tablespoon creamy peanut butter on the pieces.

Nutritional value: 189kcal, 4g protein, 28g carbs (5g fiber, 20g sugar), 8g fat (1g saturated), 14% vitamin C, 14% vitamin B3.

8. Greek Yogurt with Strawberries.

Mix 150g Greek Yogurt with 5 medium-sized strawberries cut in half.

Nutritional value: 150kcal, 11g protein, 10g carbs (10g sugar), 8g fat (5g saturated), 10% calcium, 60% vitamin C.

9. Nut Mix

Mix together 10g walnuts, 10g almond and 30g raisins.

Nutritional value: 217kcal, 4g protein, 25g carbs (2g fiber, 17g sugar), 13g fat (1g saturated), 10% magnesium.

10. Ham and Celery Sticks

Wrap 6 medium celery sticks with 3 slices of ham and serve with 1 teaspoon of whole grain mustard.

Nutritional value: 129kcal, 15g protein, 6g carbs (6g fiber), 3g fat, 12% calcium, 24% vitamin A, 12% vitamin C, 90% vitamin K, 18% vitamin B1, 12% vitamin B2, 24% vitamin B3, 15% vitamin B6, 24% vitamin B9.

11. Yogurt with Tropical Fruit

Add 150g Greek Yogurt with ½ cup cut-up kiwi and ¼ cup cut-up mango.

Nutritional value: 210kcal, 12g protein, 25g carbs (2g fiber, 19g sugar), 8g fat (5g saturated), 13% calcium, 11% vitamin A, 155% vitamin C, 46% vitamin K.

12. Blueberry Yogurt

Blend 150g low fat yogurt with ½ cup blueberries.

Nutritional value: 136kcal, 8g protein, 21g carbs (2g fiber, 18g sugar), 3g fat (1g saturated), 27% calcium, 13% vitamin C, 18% vitamin K, 21% vitamin B2, 13% vitamin B12.

13. Cup of Popcorn

Nutritional value: 31kcal, 1g protein, 6g carbs (1g fiber).

14. Roasted Chickpeas

Nutritional value 50g: 96kcal, 4g protein, 13g carbs (4g fiber, 2g sugar), 3g fat.

BODYBUILDER SHAKE RECIPES

Day 1

Breakfast: All in one shake

Energy, Muscle Gain Shake

Preparation:

Mix all the ingredients together in a juicer or blender at high speed and then enjoy a delicious shake.

We all know how hard it is to gain muscle; we always need some help with this problem. So here is a great shake to improve muscle gain and also strengthen the body. You can drink it any time of the day, but we suggest breakfast as a good time.

Ingredients:

- Milk, 400 ml
- 2 scoops Whey Protein Powder
- 2 banana 140g
- Almond oil 2 tbsp.
- 1 apple

Nutrition facts:

- Calories: 443
- Proteins: 32.5 g
- Carbs: 45 g
- Fat: 16 g

Day 2

Lunch: Get big Shake

Muscle Gain Shake

Preparation:

Mix all the ingredients together in a juicer or blender at high speed and then enjoy a delicious shake.

Eat big to get big that is the secret to building large amounts of muscle mass based mainly on a high percentage of protein's. To reach that goal you have to put a lot of effort and eat right, here is a great shake to help you with this.

Ingredients:

- ½ cup unsweetened almond milk
- 2 tbsp. maple syrup
- 2 frozen bananas
- 1 scoop whey protein powder
- 3 tbsp. of almond butter

Nutritional facts:

- Calories – 830

- Total fat- 30g (healthy fat from almond butter)
- Carbs – 115g
- Fiber- 14g
- Net Carbs -101 g
- Gluten Free
- Protein: 46 g

Day 3

Breakfast: No powder Shake

Muscle gain shake

Preparation:

Mix all the ingredients together in a juicer or blender at high speed and then enjoy a delicious shake.

Get the most out of your mix with this great recipe. Running out of time, and yet you want to achieve your nutritional quota, this delicious drink is ready in less than a minute. Your body needs a protein rich milkshake "super" for your muscles that will give you a good balance of carbohydrates and protein and what better way to do this than with this mix of ingredients.

Ingredients:

- Almond oil 2 tbsp.
- 2 tbsp. Peanut Butter
- ½ - 1 tsp Honey
- 1 medium Banana
- 2 cups Milk
- 2 scoops Whey Protein powder

Nutrition Facts:

- Calories: 601
- Protein: 49 g
- Carbs: 63 g
- Fat: 25 g

Day 4

Breakfast: Coffee Protein Shake

Muscle Gain Shake

Preparation:

Mix all the ingredients together in a juicer or blender at high speed and then enjoy a delicious shake.

This shake recipe takes seconds to make, and will be a tasty one. Make sure you use all the ingredients, blend them well and serve it after a training session. Muscle gain is one of the hardest things to achieve at the gym, so any help you can get will definitely be worth the effort.

Ingredients:

- 2 scoops Whey Protein powder
- 8 ounces Coffee
- 8 ounces 2% Milk
- 2 tbsp. Caramel Creamer

Nutrition facts:

- Calories: 398

- Protein 58.4 g
- Carbs 13.4 g
- Fat 6.4 g

Day 5

Breakfast: Peanut Butter Bulking Protein Shake

Muscle Gain Shake

Preparation:

Mix all the ingredients together in a juicer or blender at high speed and then enjoy a delicious shake.

This shake recipe is a great one to improve your performance in the gym and to increase muscle growth. Place ingredients into a blender until smooth. You might also want to use whole milk and additional peanut butter to turn this protein shake into a higher calorie weight gainer, it's up to you.

Ingredients:

- 8 oz. skim milk
- 1 banana
- 1 tbsp. peanut butter
- 2 scoops of whey protein powder

Nutritional facts:

- Calories 498

- Protein 58 g
- Carbs 44.1 g
- Fat 11 g

Day 6

Breakfast: Pink Super Shake

Muscle Gain Shake

Preparation:

Mix all the ingredients together in a juicer or blender at high speed and then enjoy a delicious shake.

When it comes to massive weight increases, it's more important to consume the right amount of calories from a proper ratio of carbohydrates to protein so you have enough energy to train and enough protein to allow your muscles to develop.

Ingredients:

- ¾ cup organic frozen raspberries
- ½ small banana
- 1 scoop whey protein powder
- ½ tbsp. raw coconut butter
- 5 g glutamine
- 1 cup spring water

Nutritional facts:

- Calories: 268
- Protein : 16.5 g
- Carbs: 44.5 g
- Fat 6.7 g

Day 7

Breakfast: Banana Protein Shake

Muscle Gain Shake

Proteins are the most important nutrients for muscle growth. They ensure that the body functions properly. For practitioners of bodybuilding, they allow you to have bigger muscles provided, of course, you follow appropriate training, and you have a healthy diet. This is an easy-to-prepare shake that has a large amount of protein.

Preparation:

Mix all the ingredients together in a juicer or blender at high speed and then enjoy a delicious shake.

Ingredients:

- 8 oz. skim milk
- 1 banana
- ½ cups of oats
- 2 scoops of whey protein powder

Nutritional facts:

- Calories 554
- Protein 58g
- Carbs 67.5g
- Fat 6g

Day 8

Breakfast: Banana Berry Protein Shake

Gaining Mass Protein shake

This is a great shake for gaining strength and mass in a short period of time, with no delays. It's healthy, natural, and will make a big impact in your gym routine. So let's see the ingredients and all that it has to offer you.

Preparation:

Mix all the ingredients together in a juicer or blender at high speed and then enjoy a delicious shake.

Ingredients:

- 12 ounces of water
- 4 ice cubes
- 1 banana
- 2 scoops of whey protein

Nutritional facts:

- Calories 314

- Protein 45.1g
- Carbs: 32.1g
- Fat 2.4g

Day 9

Breakfast: Almond and Banana Thirst

Gaining Mass Shake

Increase your muscle gain using this shake recipe, and then track your progress the day after you've trained to see if it helped your performance. You could even prepare it the night before in order to make all the ingredients combine even better.

Preparation:

Mix all the ingredients together in a juicer or blender at high speed and then enjoy a delicious shake.

Ingredients:

- 1 frozen medium banana
- 1 cup plain yogurt
- 100 ml ice cold water
- 1 ounce ground almonds
- 1 cup raw oats

Nutritional facts:

- Calories: 650

- Protein: 53 g
- Carbs: 75 g
- Fat: 15 g

Day 10

Lunch: Cinnamon Protein Shake

Gaining Muscle Shake

Follow this shake recipe to increase your muscle gain, with a low fat intake. You can drink this shake any time of the day.

Preparation:

Mix all the ingredients together in a juicer or blender at high speed and then enjoy a delicious shake.

Ingredients:

- 1 cup Skim Milk
- 1 frozen Banana
- 1 scoop Whey Protein Powder
- 1 tbsp. Peanut Butter

Nutritional Facts:

- Calories: 391
- Protein: 38g
- Carbs: 42.1g
- Fat: 10g

Day 11

Breakfast: Heavy gainer Shake

Gaining Mass Shake

Here is a great shake recipe that will give you a huge boost of energy and also will help increasing your muscle development. So be ready for a great experience that will improve your gym sessions.

Preparation:

Mix all the ingredients together in a juicer or blender at high speed and then enjoy a delicious shake.

Ingredients:

- 10-14 oz. pure water
- 1/2 cup raw almonds
- 1/2 large frozen banana
- 2 scoops whey protein powder

Nutritional facts:

- Calories: 380
- Proteins: 75 g

- Carbs: 57 g
- Fat: 15 g

Day 12

Breakfast: Extreme Energy Shake

Gaining mass and energy Shake

If you were looking for something to supply you with some extra energy and also improve your muscle growth you should go for this shake recipe. This shake is full of healthy ingredients. Green Tea has been said to prevent cancer and flax seeds provide a good serving of omega 3 which is important for your body's development.

Preparation:

Mix all the ingredients together in a juicer or blender at high speed and then enjoy a delicious shake.

Ingredients:

- 10 oz. pure water
- 10 strawberries (Fresh or Frozen)
- 1 tbs. flax-seed oil
- 1/2 tsp Green Tea Powder
- 1/2 tsp vanilla extract
- 1 scoop Whey Protein Powder

Nutritional Facts:

- Calories: 420
- Protein: 50 g
- Carbs: 42 g
- Fat: 17 g

Day 13

Lunch: Peaches Shake

Gaining muscle Shake

The peaches in this shake give it a great flavor and cottage cheese is an excellent source of protein and is easy to digest. The best time of the day to drink this shake would be in the morning but you can drink it any time.

Preparation:

Mix all the ingredients together in a juicer or blender at high speed and then enjoy a delicious shake.

Ingredients:

- 8 oz. pure water
- 1 ripe peach
- 2 tbs. low-fat cottage cheese
- Brown sugar
- 1.5 scoop whey protein powder

Nutritional Facts:

- Calories: 250

- Proteins: 40 g
- Carbs: 21 g
- Fat: 8 g

Day 14

Breakfast: Blueberry Shake

Gaining muscle Shake

Let's start the day off with a great shake recipe that will maintain your energy levels high, and provide the required protein intake so you can increase more muscle in a shorter time period. Blueberries are known to be great antioxidants and help prevent cancer.

Preparation:

Mix all the ingredients together in a juicer or blender at high speed and then enjoy a delicious shake.

Ingredients:

- 10 oz. Pure water
- 1/2 cup fresh or frozen blueberries
- 1.5 scoop whey protein powder
- 2 tsp. flax-seed oil

Nutritional Facts:

- Calories: 210 g

- Proteins: 39g
- Carbs: 22 g
- Fat: 4 g

Day 15

Breakfast: Strawberry Shake

Gaining muscle Shake

There is no better way of getting fast results when trying to get muscle growth, than using shakes and this shake recipe will taste delicious because of the combination of strawberries and cottage cheese.

Preparation:

Mix all the ingredients together in a juicer or blender at high speed and then enjoy a delicious shake.

Ingredients:

- 10 oz. pure water
- 8 frozen strawberries
- 4 tbs. low-fat cottage cheese
- 1.5 scoop whey protein powder

Nutritional Facts:

- Calories: 310 g
- Proteins: 51g

- Carbs: 27g
- Fat: 7 g

Day 16

Breakfast: Banana delight Shake

Gaining muscle Shake

Combine the following ingredients to get a shake high in omega 3 and high in potassium to help you increase muscle gain, and also maintain a healthy body.

Preparation:

Mix all the ingredients together in a juicer or blender at high speed and then enjoy a delicious shake.

Ingredients:

- 8 oz. pure water
- 1/2 banana (frozen)
- 2 scoops whey protein powder
- 2 tsp. flax-seed oil

Nutritional Facts:

- Calories: 350 g
- Proteins: 65g
- Carbs: 29g

- Fat: 9 g

Day 17

Breakfast: Pineapple Shake

Gaining muscle Shake

Try this amazing shake recipe that is well known for fast results and delicious taste. It's perfect to help you increase your muscle gain, and will have a strong effect on your immune system.

Preparation:

Mix all the ingredients together in a juicer or blender at high speed and then enjoy a delicious shake.

Ingredients:

- 1 cup of pineapple juice
- 3 strawberries
- 1 banana
- 1 tsp. of yogurt
- 1 scoop whey protein powder

Nutritional Facts:

- Calories: 340 g
- Proteins: 63g

- Carbs: 27g
- Fat: 10 g

Day 18

Breakfast: Muscle Shake

Gaining muscle Shake

Having problems getting bigger muscles? If the answer is yes, you should try this shake recipe that will bring instant results in your training and energy throughout the day.

Preparation:

Mix all the ingredients together in a juicer or blender at high speed and then enjoy a delicious shake.

Ingredients:

- 1 c. low-fat milk
- 1/2 c. plain low-fat yogurt
- 1 banana, sliced
- 2 tbsp. Whey Protein Powder
- 6 strawberries, sliced
- 1 tsp. wheat germ
- 1 tbsp. honey or maple syrup
- 1/4 cup of any frozen berries

- Pinch of nutmeg or carob powder

Nutritional Facts:

- Calories: 600
- Proteins: 70g
- Carbs: 54g
- Fat: 15 g

Day 19

Breakfast: Oatmeal Shake

Gaining muscle Shake

This is a great shake recipe to increase muscle mass and protect your heart. It will help you stay alert during the entire day, go for it.

Preparation:

Mix all the ingredients together in a juicer or blender at high speed and then enjoy a delicious shake.

Ingredients:

- 2 scoops whey protein powder
- 1 cup sugar-free vanilla ice cream
- 1 cup oatmeal
- 2 cups non-fat milk
- 1.2 cup water
- A splash of peppermint extract!

Nutritional Facts:

- Calories: 621
- Proteins: 65g
- Carbs: 58g
- Fat: 22 g

Day 20

Lunch: Tropical Shake

Gaining muscle Shake

This is one of the most delicious shakes I have ever tasted and I am sure you will enjoy it. The mix between banana, pineapple, and coconut gives it a tropical flavor that should go well in the morning or mid-morning. The bananas don't have to be frozen, they can be room temperature but some people prefer that it be cold if they have just finished working out.

Preparation:

Mix all the ingredients together in a juicer or blender at high speed and then enjoy a delicious shake.

Ingredients:

- 8 oz. pure water
- 1/2 tsp. pineapple extract
- 1/2 tsp. coconut extract
- 1 tbsp. cottage cheese
- 1/2 frozen banana

Nutritional Facts:

- Calories: 540
- Proteins: 25g
- Carbs: 43g
- Fat: 17g

Day 21

Lunch: Fruit Shake

Gaining muscle Shake

Protein is the key to muscle growth and recovery. Make sure you try this shake at any time of the day. This berry shake has many antioxidant qualities that will benefit you as you age and will prevent you from getting sick as often and that can be very important when you can't afford to take week long breaks from working out.

Preparation:

Mix all the ingredients together in a juicer or blender at high speed and then enjoy a delicious shake.

Ingredients:

- 2 scoops Milk protein powder
- 4 large strawberries
- blueberries (a small handful)
- water (just a few drops)
- 3 eggs

Nutritional Facts:

- Calories: 470
- Proteins: 45g
- Carbs: 39g
- Fat: 15g

Day 22

Breakfast: Apple Pie Delight Shake

Muscle gain Shake

Athletes who consume more protein will increase more muscle mass than sedentary people because they maximize growth potential so try to make sure you add this shake just before or just after a training session. The mixture of flavors from apple, cinnamon, and nutmeg give an original flavor not normally found in other shakes.

Preparation:

Mix all the ingredients together in a juicer or blender at high speed and then enjoy a delicious shake.

Ingredients:

- 1 scoop Whey protein powder
- 1 peeled and cored apple, cut into pieces
- 1 1/2 cups of milk
- 1/2 tsp cinnamon
- 1/2 tsp nutmeg
- 5 Ice Cubes

Nutritional Facts:

- Calories: 350
- Proteins: 35g
- Carbs: 21g
- Fat: 10g

Day 23

Breakfast: Pumpkin Shake

Low on carbs Shake

Here's one shake for you that's a great source of protein and provides a high level of energy during the day. The flax oil and yogurt provide you with several ingredients for your bodies overall function and help give this shake a boost of calcium and omega 3.

Preparation:

Mix all the ingredients together in a juicer or blender at high speed and then enjoy a delicious shake.

Ingredients:

- 2 Scoops Milk protein powder
- 8 oz. water
- 1 tbsp. Flax oil
- 1 tsp. Pumpkin pie spice
- 8 oz. Yogurt
- 4-6 ice cubes

Nutritional Facts:

- Calories: 300
- Proteins: 40g
- Carbs: 26g
- Fat: 11g

Day 24

Breakfast: Cinnamon Shake

Muscle gain Shake

This shake should be consumed early in the morning before a training session because it's a good energy provider and will also help accelerate muscle recovery.

Preparation:

Mix all the ingredients together in a juicer or blender at high speed and then enjoy a delicious shake.

Ingredients:

- 1 graham cracker
- 1/2 tsp cinnamon
- vanilla extract
- 12oz. water
- 4 Ice Cubes

Nutritional Facts:

- Calories: 280
- Proteins: 10g

- Carbs: 15g
- Fat: 5g

Day 25

Breakfast: Peanut Butter and Banana Shake

Muscle gain Shake

Peanut butter is a great source of protein and energy. Many athletes use peanut butter as a main source of energy before training or before competing. The banana and almond content improve the flavor and make it even more digestive.

Preparation:

Mix all the ingredients together in a juicer or blender at high speed and then enjoy a delicious shake.

Ingredients:

- 2 scoops Whey Protein Powder
- 100g almond slices
- 1 tbsp. peanut butter
- 500ml skim milk
- half banana
- 1 table-spoon honey

Nutritional Facts:

- Calories: 600
- Proteins: 55g
- Carbs: 35g
- Fat: 10g

Day 26

Breakfast: Super Mix Shake

Muscle gain Shake

Depending on your metabolism, you will adapt to some of the shakes better than others. For those of you who prefer a sweeter flavor in your shakes, this is a good choice. You can adapt certain ingredients to change the flavor to your preference like the caramel, hazelnuts, or vanilla yogurt.

Preparation:

Mix all the ingredients together in a juicer or blender at high speed and then enjoy a delicious shake.

Ingredients:

- 10 Ice Cubes
- 12 oz. fat-free milk
- 2 tbsp. fat free vanilla yogurt or Kefir
- 1 tbsp. reduced fat peanut butter
- 2 tbsp. spoon hazelnuts
- 1 tbsp. caramel ice cream topping

Nutritional Facts:

- Calories: 430
- Proteins: 23g
- Carbs: 20g
- Fat: 11g

Day 27

Breakfast: Lean mass Banana Shake

Muscle gain Shake

People who stick to a muscle gain diet or routine will benefit even more if they add muscle shakes because of the ease of preparation and because of how fast the body can absorb the protein and nutrients.

Preparation:

Mix all the ingredients together in a juicer or blender at high speed and then enjoy a delicious shake.

Ingredients:

- 1/2 frozen banana
- 2 tbsp. Whipping cream (heavy cream, not cream out of a can)
- 2 eggs
- 10-12 oz. water
- 4-6 ice cubes

Nutritional Facts:

- Calories: 320
- Proteins: 18g
- Carbs: 15g
- Fat: 9g

Day 28

Lunch: Sweet Boost Shake

Muscle gain Shake

Here is a great example of a shake recipe that has very different ingredients, but combined they are a great source of protein and will increase your gym performance.

Preparation:

Mix all the ingredients together in a juicer or blender at high speed and then enjoy a delicious shake.

Ingredients:

- 1 medium to large banana
- 8 oz. light Milk
- 1 tbsp. Flaxseed and Almond Mixture
- 1 tsp Maple Syrup
- Few drops of vanilla essence/extract
- 3-4 cubes ice
- 1 tbsp. low-fat natural yogurt

Nutritional Facts:

- Calories: 450
- Proteins: 19g
- Carbs: 16g
- Fat: 10g

Day 29

Breakfast: Orange Shake

Muscle gain Shake

Let's start the day with an awesome shake to boost our immune system and help you increase more muscle. This recipe is high in vitamin C and potassium because of the strawberries and orange juice which will also allow your muscles to recover faster.

Preparation:

Mix all the ingredients together in a juicer or blender at high speed and then enjoy a delicious shake.

Ingredients:

- 8 oz. Orange Juice
- 4-5 ice cubes
- 1 tsp. Vanilla Extract
- ½ banana
- 2-3 frozen strawberries
- 2 tsp. honey

Nutritional Facts:

- Calories: 291
- Proteins: 15g
- Carbs: 12g
- Fat: 5g

Day 30

Breakfast: Almond Shake Blast

Muscle gain Shake

Plan on having a better digestion after having this shake with this combination of oatmeal, raisins, almonds, and peanut butter. The raisins give it a great flavor and the oatmeal gives it a different texture than other shakes.

Preparation:

Mix all the ingredients together in a juicer or blender at high speed and then enjoy a delicious shake.

Ingredients:

- 10-12 oz. of skim milk
- 1.2 cup of raw oatmeal
- 1.2 cup of raisins
- 12 shredded almonds
- 1 tbsp. of peanut butter.

Nutritional Facts:

- Calories: 380

- Proteins: 18g
- Carbs: 15g
- Fat: 12g

Day 31

Breakfast: Wild berry Shake

Muscle Gain Shake

Raspberries are known to be very high on vitamin C and antioxidants which many medical professionals suggest as an anti-cancer supplement to your normal day to day foods and meals. It's the perfect mixture for those who want to gain muscle mass and strength. You can replace an ordinary snack with this healthy drink that is not very high on protein but will help take a break from all the other high protein shakes you will be taking on a daily basis.

Preparation:

Mix all the ingredients together in a juicer or blender at high speed and then enjoy a delicious shake.

Ingredients:

- 8 raspberries
- 4 strawberries
- 15 blueberries
- 16 ounces non-fat milk
- 1/2 cup ice cubes

Nutritional Facts:

- Calories: 210
- Proteins: 9g
- Carbs: 10g
- Fat: 8g

Day 32

Breakfast: Peanut Banana Shake

Muscle Gain Shake

In terms of nutrition this shake is high on lean protein and complex carbs, so it will increase muscle growth and recovery. It will also give you an energy boost while your training if you drink it half hour before.

Preparation:

Mix all the ingredients together in a juicer or blender at high speed and then enjoy a delicious shake.

Ingredients:

- ½ cup Peanuts
- 1/2 Banana
- 1 Cup Skim Milk
- 1/4 Cup Quaker Oats
- 2 Ice Cubes
- Pinch of Salt

Nutritional Facts:

- Calories: 230
- Proteins: 18g
- Carbs: 12g
- Fat: 5g

Day 33

Breakfast: Carrot Pineapple Shake

Muscle Gain Shake

This shake might look a little strange for you guys, but believe me it's a good one for you and your body. You can remove or lower the portions for some of the ingredients depending on your preference as this mix is very different from some of the others.

Preparation:

Mix all the ingredients together in a juicer or blender at high speed and then enjoy a delicious shake.

Ingredients:

- 1 cup chocolate milk
- 3/4 c shredded carrots
- 10 frozen pineapple chunks
- 2 tsp unsweetened shredded coconut
- 1 tsp vanilla
- 1 tsp sweet cream
- 4 oz. Neufchatel Cheese or cream cheese

Nutritional Facts:

- Calories: 220
- Proteins: 21g
- Carbs: 13g
- Fat: 13g

Day 34

Lunch: Pumpkin Shake

Muscle Gain Shake

Great shake recipe to help you increase your muscle gain and strength with a very unique taste that makes it fun to drink while still consuming a decent amount of protein. It's the perfect supplement for muscle recovery and muscle gain.

Preparation:

Mix all the ingredients together in a juicer or blender at high speed and then enjoy a delicious shake.

Ingredients:

- 3/4 c. milk (whatever kind you like)
- 1/4 c. canned pumpkin
- 1 tbsp. Pumpkin Pie flavored syrup
- 1/2 tsp. pumpkin pie spice
- 10 ice cubes

Nutritional Facts:

- Calories: 235

- Proteins: 20g
- Carbs: 17g
- Fat: 1.5g

Day 35

Breakfast: Blueberry Apple Shake

Energy Boost Shake

Maintaining a high level of energy is the goal of this shake. It will also provide you with some lean proteins that will help you even if you're a bit tired that day or if you just want to push yourself harder that day.

Preparation:

Mix all the ingredients together in a juicer or blender at high speed and then enjoy a delicious shake.

Ingredients:

- 1/2 small apple cut into small pieces (with skin)
- 1/2 cup cherries (dark, sweet, pitted)
- 1/2 cup blueberries
- 4 tbsp. wheat germ
- ice cubes (if desired)
- 1/2 cup whey protein

Nutritional Facts:

- Calories: 300
- Proteins: 39g
- Carbs: 18g
- Fat: 5g

Day 36

Breakfast: Cherry Banana Energy Boost Shake

Two great tasting ingredients in one shake. Cherries and bananas are provide a great source of fiber that your body needs when taking in large portions of protein. Try this drink before any training session night or day.

Preparation:

Mix all the ingredients together in a juicer or blender at high speed and then enjoy a delicious shake.

Ingredients:

- 1/2 cup cherries (dark, sweet, pitted)
- 1/2 cup Banana
- 4 tbsp. wheat germ
- ice cubes (if desired)
- 1/2 cup whey protein

Nutritional Facts:

- Calories:300

- Proteins: 39g
- Carbs: 18g
- Fat: 5g

Day 37

Breakfast: Egg Mania Shake

Muscle Gain Shake

You can have a muscle gain shake recipe with no protein powder in it and still intake a good amount of protein. The chick peas give it a green color but don't really change the flavor at all. This is a great combination of proteins and carbs.

Preparation:

Mix all the ingredients together in a juicer or blender at high speed and then enjoy a delicious shake.

Ingredients:

- 4 egg whites
- 1/2 cup cottage cheese
- 1 banana
- 1/4 cup chick peas
- pineapple slices
- Coconut milk
- Coconut extract can be added
- ice cubes

Nutritional Facts:

- Calories: 280
- Proteins: 25g
- Carbs: 40g
- Fat: 4g

Day 38

Breakfast: High Protein Shake

Muscle Gain Shake

Increase your gym performance by increase the amounts of protein you have on a daily basis. This shake is high on protein and high on flavor.

Preparation:

Mix all the ingredients together in a juicer or blender at high speed and then enjoy a delicious shake.

Ingredients:

- 1/2 c water
- 1 scoop Whey Protein Powder
- 2 tbsp. Honey
- 1 tbsp. Smooth Peanut Butter
- 1/2 cup Ice

Nutritional Facts:

- Calories:114
- Proteins: 34g

- Carbs: 5.2g
- Fat: 4.5g

Day 39

Breakfast: Fruit Mix Shake

Muscle Gain Shake

This shake recipe can easily replace your breakfast but this still have a healthy portion of food to nourish your body. It has a lot of the nutrients your body needs to have a good start in the morning. Protein and carbs are included in this recipe to give your energy and strength when training.

Preparation:

Mix all the ingredients together in a juicer or blender at high speed and then enjoy a delicious shake.

Ingredients:

- 1/2 banana chopped
- 1/2 cup of chopped strawberries
- 1 small apple
- 1 small plum
- 1 cup of chocolate milk
- 1 tbsp. of smooth peanut butter
- 1 scoop Whey Protein Powder

Nutritional Facts:

- Calories: 700
- Proteins: 46g
- Carbs: 90g
- Fat: 20g

Day 40

Breakfast: Choco Shake

Muscle Gain Shake

A great way of combining a dark chocolate bar with the right ingredients to obtain a shake that will increase your gym performance and muscle gain.

Preparation:

Mix all the ingredients together in a juicer or blender at high speed and then enjoy a delicious shake.

Ingredients:

- 1 dark chocolate bar
- 4 eggs
- 3 cups milk
- 1 scoop Whey Protein Powder

Nutritional Facts:

- Calories: 290
- Proteins: 45g
- Carbs: 37g

- Fat: 19g

Day 41

Breakfast: Taste of Everything Shake

Muscle Gain Shake

This shake recipe is an excellent source of protein and fiber your body needs. It's full of nutrients and vitamins that will you both bigger muscles and more energy when training to build more muscles.

Preparation:

Mix all the ingredients together in a juicer or blender at high speed and then enjoy a delicious shake.

Ingredients:

- Grapes, 4 grapes, seedless
- Blackberries, fresh, 0.5 grams
- Blueberries, fresh, 25 berries
- Strawberries, fresh, 0.5 grams
- Pineapple, fresh, 1 slice, thin (3-1/2" diameter x 1/2" thick
- Apples, fresh, 10 grams
- Yogurt, plain, low fat, 0.5 container (4 oz.)
- Kale, 0.5 grams

- Broccoli, fresh, 1 stalk
- Oranges, 0.5 grams
- 1 scoop Whey Protein Powder

Nutritional Facts:

- Calories: 280
- Proteins: 48g
- Carbs: 31g
- Fat: 4.2g

Day 42

Breakfast: Wake up Now Shake

Muscle Gain Shake

Here is how you should start the day, energy will be the defining word for this shake, but don't think it's not good for gaining muscle too, because you would be wrong.

Preparation:

Mix all the ingredients together in a juicer or blender at high speed and then enjoy a delicious shake.

Ingredients:

- 1 fresh banana, medium
- 2 servings (60 grs) oat flakes
- 1-2 tbsp. peanut butter, smooth style
- 1 cup (250 ml) yogurt, plain, low fat (0% - 1.5% mf)
- 0.5 tbsp. (or less) cinnamon, ground

Nutritional Facts:

- Calories: 650
- Proteins: 28g

- Carbs: 85g
- Fat: 10g

Day 43

Lunch: Mango Tango Shake

Muscle Gain Shake

This is a great shake you can add to other days so you can take two shakes per day since it is high on fiber and low on fat. This lean shake will help you fight any tiredness in the gym and will improve your performance.

Preparation:

Mix all the ingredients together in a juicer or blender at high speed and then enjoy a delicious shake.

Ingredients:

- 2 large strawberries, fresh or frozen
- 10 blueberries, fresh or frozen
- 1 cup Orange Juice
- 1/2 mango, fresh or frozen
- 1 scoop Milk Protein Powder

Nutritional Facts:

- Calories: 250

- Proteins: 30.5g
- Carbs: 52g
- Fat: 8.4g

Day 44

Breakfast: Pineapple Tangerine Shake

Muscle Gain Shake

To gain muscle, there is no secret; you have to train and eat right! You will struggle if you don't have enough energy while training and that's why adding ingredients that will give you a boost when necessary will make all the difference when trying to build stronger muscles.

Preparation:

Mix all the ingredients together in a juicer or blender at high speed and then enjoy a delicious shake.

Ingredients:

- 1/2 cup Pineapple, frozen chunks
- 1/2 cup Tangerines, (mandarin oranges), canned
- 2 tsp. honey
- 1 scoop Whey Protein Powder

Nutritional Facts:

- Calories:150

- Proteins: 39g
- Carbs: 17g
- Fat: 11g

Day 45

Breakfast: Peanut Butter Apple Shake

Muscle Gain Shake

Shakes can be a great source of calories and energy which are necessary to increase muscle mass. This delicious shake recipe is made to help you increase your muscle gain and maintain a high level of energy.

Preparation:

Mix all the ingredients together in a juicer or blender at high speed and then enjoy a delicious shake.

Ingredients:

- 3/4 Cup plain or vanilla yogurt
- 2 tbsp. Peanut Butter
- 1 Banana
- 1/8 Cup milk
- 3/4 Cup ice
- 1 apple

Nutritional Facts:

- Calories: 440
- Proteins: 22g
- Carbs: 50g
- Fat: 19g

Day 46

Breakfast: Banana Super Shake

Muscle Gain Shake

Vanilla almond milk will make this a great protein shake. It promotes muscle mass growth without unbalancing your diet. You can reduce or eliminate the cinnamon to make it to your specific preference.

Preparation:

Mix all the ingredients together in a juicer or blender at high speed and then enjoy a delicious shake.

Ingredients:

- 1/2 cup vanilla almond milk
- 1/2 cup water
- 1/2 banana
- Dash of cinnamon
- 1 scoop of vanilla protein powder

Nutritional Facts:

- Calories:350

- Proteins: 43g
- Carbs: 25g
- Fat: 5g

Day 47

Breakfast: Dark Oat Power Shake

Muscle Gain Shake

The combination of dark chocolate, cottage cheese, and oatmeal will increase your muscle development, and get you that energy boost that you were looking for in the gym while improve digestion and strengthening your heart.

Preparation:

Mix all the ingredients together in a juicer or blender at high speed and then enjoy a delicious shake.

Ingredients:

- 1/2 cup of Cottage Cheese (or 1 cup Greek yoghurt)
- 1/2 - 1 cup water (depending on desired thickness) or milk
- 10g dark chocolate
- ½ cup raw oatmeal
- 1/2 banana
- 1 scoop Whey Protein Powder

Nutritional Facts:

- Calories: 150
- Proteins: 40g
- Carbs: 20g
- Fat: 8g

Day 48

Breakfast: Milk Protein Shake

Muscle Gain Shake

To build and maintain your muscle mass you need to increase carbohydrates and protein so that you have the energy to work hard and the ingredients to allow your muscles to fully develop.

Preparation:

Mix all the ingredients together in a juicer or blender at high speed and then enjoy a delicious shake.

Ingredients:

- 1 scoop Milk protein powder
- 1/2 bananas
- 1/2 cup almond slices
- 8 oz milk
- 3 ice cubes

Nutritional Facts:

- Calories: 335
- Proteins: 31g

- Carbs: 25g
- Fat: 18g

Day 49

Breakfast: Avocado Shake

Muscle Gain Shake

Protein shakes with vegetables are uncommon but should be more normal because of the value they bring to your diet and to your body. Avocado is considered by some as a "super food" and is great for your body.

Preparation:

Mix all the ingredients together in a juicer or blender at high speed and then enjoy a delicious shake.

Ingredients:

- 1/2 avocado
- 1 tbsp. shredded coconut
- 1 cup almond milk
- 1 scoop Whey Protein Powder

Nutritional Facts:

- Calories: 300
- Proteins: 35g

- Carbs: 20g
- Fat: 8g

Day 50

Breakfast: Very Berry Shake

Muscle Gain Shake

A complete berry and protein combination to improve muscle growth and recovery all in one shake. The taste is magnificent and the results are even better when you need to train hard and want to see results.

Preparation:

Mix all the ingredients together in a juicer or blender at high speed and then enjoy a delicious shake.

Ingredients:

- ½ cup strawberries
- ¼ cup mixed berries (raspberries, blueberries and blackberries)
- ¼ cup organic pomegranate juice
- ¼ cup organic grape juice
- handful sliced almonds for topping
- 1 scoop Whey Protein Powder

Nutritional Facts:

- Calories: 200
- Proteins: 31g
- Carbs: 19g
- Fat: 1g

OTHER GREAT TITLES BY THIS AUTHOR

Advanced Mental Toughness Training for Bodybuilders

Using Visualization to Push Yourself to the Limit

By

Joseph Correa

Certified Sports Nutritionist

Becoming Mentally Tougher in Bodybuilding by Using Meditation

Reach Your Potential by Controlling Your Inner Thoughts

By

Joseph Correa

Certified Sports Nutritionist

www.ingramcontent.com/pod-product-compliance
Lightning Source LLC
Chambersburg PA
CBHW070136080526
44586CB00015B/1722